Inventions That Shaped the World

THE Telephone

PATRICIA K. KUMMER

Franklin Watts
A Division of Scholastic Inc.
New York • Toronto • London • Auckland • Sydney
Mexico City • New Delhi • Hong Kong
Danbury, Connecticut

Photographs © 2006: Art Resource, NY/Bridgeman-Giraudon: cover bottom left; Corbis Images: 31, 43 (Bettmann), 40; Getty Images/Hulton Archive: 52 (MPI), 8 (Stock Montage), 16 (Arthur Tanner), 11, 20, 23, 65; Library of Congress: 25, 26, 32, 34, 38, 63; National Geographic Image Collection/Bell Family: 36; Photo Researchers, NY/J-L Charmet/SPL: 46; PhotoEdit/David Young-Wolff: cover top left, chapter openers; Superstock, Inc.: 5 (Roderick Chen), 14 (John Mix Stanley/David David Gallery); The Art Archive/Picture Desk: cover bottom right (Culver Pictures), chapter openers, cover top right (Dagli Orti); The Image Works: 6 (Bob Daemmrich), 17 (Mary Evans Picture Library), 48 (SSPL), 56 (Mitch Wojnarowicz/Amsterdam Recorder).

Illustration by J. T. Morrow

Cover design by The Design Lab
Book production by The Design Lab

Library of Congress Cataloging-in-Publication Data
Kummer, Patricia K.
  The telephone / Patricia K. Kummer.
     p. cm. — (Inventions that shaped the world)
  Includes bibliographical references and index.
  ISBN 0-531-12407-X (lib. bdg.)   0-531-13903-4 (pbk.)
  1. Telephone—Juvenile literature. I. Title. II. Series.
  TK6165.K86 2005
  621.385—dc22   2005009958

Contents

Long-Distance Communication

How do you let your parents know that you've decided to stay after school to work on a project, or that you'll need a ride home? You probably call them on the telephone. Perhaps you use a prepaid phone card at a pay phone, or maybe you have your own cell phone. How do you share news with friends or relatives who have moved to other parts of the country? You might make a long-distance

Almost every home in the United States has at least one telephone.

5

phone call, but maybe you send an e-mail. How do you find the most up-to-date information for a school report? What do your parents use to help them plan a family vacation? You and your parents probably use the Internet. Telephone calls, e-mails, and the Internet are some of the ways we carry out long-distance communications today. All of these forms of communication send messages through wired or wireless telephone systems.

An office manager uses a fax machine to send a customer a copy of a document.

Long-distance communication is not limited to phone calls to people in other states or countries. It includes all communication that takes place over any distance—down the street, in the next town, or around the world. Another word for communication over distance is *telecommunication*. *Tele* is the Greek word for "from afar" or "a distance."

The Importance of Communication

When we *communicate,* we send information or request information from others. Through communication, we can also share our thoughts and feelings with others. For communication to be complete, however, four things must happen. First, the message must reach the other person. Second, the message must be clearly understood. Third, the message must arrive in a timely manner. Fourth, the other person should be able to respond quickly.

When people talk face-to-face or across a room, these communication requirements are easily met. But what happens if the person with whom you want to communicate is some distance away—across the street, a few miles away, or in another state or country? You could walk down the street or send a letter through the mail. Both of those methods take time, and with a letter you won't receive an immediate response.

For hundreds of years, scientists and inventors worked to develop a way to fulfill these four requirements of communicating across long distances. With the invention of the telephone, all four of those communication requirements were met. The word *telephone* comes from two Greek words: *tele*, and *phone*, which means "sound." Simply stated, the telephone is a machine, or a method, that can send sound over distances.

Alexander Graham Bell was an educator as well as an inventor.

The Need to Communicate

From the beginning of human life, people have tried to communicate with one another. Hand and facial gestures probably sent the first messages. Even now, when we don't understand someone's language, we rely on sign language to get our meaning across. Early people also used different tones and levels of loudness in their voices to communicate. From these sounds, spoken languages evolved. Eventually, written languages developed. Then people could communicate through letters, books, and newspapers.

From the earliest times, people wanted to improve the way they communicated. They invented new ways of getting their messages delivered faster and across greater distances. They used smoke, fire, drums, and bells. They used runners, messengers on horseback, stagecoaches, railroads, and telegraphs. By the mid-1800s, some scientists thought about sending messages from the human voice over long distances by using electricity and wires. Finally, an inventor named Alexander Graham Bell came along. He understood how the human ear and voice worked. Bell used that knowledge and learned enough about electricity to invent the telephone in 1876.

The Invention Process

Because the telephone plays such an important part in our lives today, it's hard to believe that it took so long to be invented. Imagine what life would be like without telephones, fax machines, and computer modems. How would people call for help in emergencies? How would businesses order supplies from factories? How would you order flowers for your mother's birthday? How would you find the best bus route from your home to a local museum? The telephone, like many other inventions, came about because the time was right.

An invention usually arises from a need or from a desire to do something more easily or to make life better. Someone with imagination and curiosity (an inventor) begins to think about making a product or developing a process (an invention). Work on an invention can take many years. Because inventors usually experience many failures before they have a successful invention, they must have patience and determination.

Sometimes inventions occur when two or more people work together. Other inventions have developed in separate parts of the world either at about the same time or at different times. This has happened because people in various parts of the world experienced the same needs. In the years before speedy transportation and instant communication, similar inventions or steps toward an invention occurred independently in different places.

A new invention usually develops as a result of an earlier invention or idea. For example, in the early 1800s, Eli Whitney used the idea of interchangeable parts to develop a process of mass production. In this way, he was able to fill an order of ten thousand muskets for the U.S. government. About a hundred years later, Henry Ford invented the assembly line to mass-produce Model T Fords. These automobiles were made with interchangeable parts. The development of the first telephone resulted from attempts to build a better telegraph.

The assembly line was created by Henry Ford to mass produce Model T Ford automobiles.

Inventions Affect Daily Life

If an invention is truly useful, it becomes an important part of daily life. When this happens, improvements are made to the original product or to how the product is made. This is true of the telephone. For example, telephones now come in a variety of sizes, shapes, and colors. Also, the process of making and receiving phone calls has changed over the years. In addition, the materials over which calls are sent across the country and around the world have improved.

Today, the telephone is regarded as a necessity. The percentage of people who have phone service is even one of the measures of a country's economic strength. Each year, this percentage increases. In the United States, most homes have one telephone line, but phones and computers in several rooms can be connected to that line. At an early age, American children memorize their home phone numbers and are taught how to use the telephone. They learn how to dial 911 in case of an emergency. Businesses have several lines and use them for telephone, fax, and Internet connections. A phrase in a major telephone company's advertisement once told people to "Reach out and touch someone." The continued improvements in telephones and telephone service make it easier, faster, more convenient, and less expensive to reach people almost anywhere in the world.

Smoke Signals, Drumbeats, Dots and Dashes

For thousands of years, people have been devising ways to communicate with one another from great distances. They've used bonfires, smoke signals, drums, bells, pigeons, riders on horseback, and electric wires. Most of these methods took a great deal of time and effort from many people and were only used in emergencies or to announce important events.

As Far As the Eye Can See

The eye can see farther than the ear can hear. Because of this, many early messages were sent by visual signals. Some of these visual signals could be seen up to 60 miles (97 kilometers) away. Visual signals, however, had to be sent from high hilltops because Earth's natural curve limits the distance at which these signals can be seen.

Early Chinese, Egyptians, and Romans lit lines of bonfires to send messages of warning from Point A to Point Z. When the people at Point B saw the light from the bonfire at Point A, they would light their fire, then the people at Point C would light theirs. This would occur until the last bonfire was lit and the message was received at Point Z. In

American Indians and many other groups throughout history used smoke signals to send messages.

1588, the English lit bonfires to let Queen Elizabeth I know that the huge Spanish invasion fleet was approaching. The bonfires sent the message about 250 miles (402 km) from the coast of Cornwall to London within a short amount of time. It would have taken a rider on horseback about twenty hours to travel that distance. The message from the early warning system helped the English defeat the Spanish fleet. This system does have some drawbacks. Bonfires are seen best at night and don't work well in rainy or foggy weather.

Smoke signals have been used since early Roman times. The best-known senders of smoke signals were Native Americans on the Great Plains. They would build a smoky fire on a hill. Then they would release puffs of smoke by covering and uncovering the fire with a blanket. Different numbers of puffs meant different things. The smoke could be seen up to 60 miles (97 km) away. Smoke signals also have drawbacks. They are seen best during the day, don't work well in rainy or foggy weather, and are affected by wind.

From at least 405 B.C., people have sent messages by reflecting sunlight from shiny surfaces, such as glass, a mirror, or polished metal. Greek soldiers sent messages during battle using their shiny shields. In 1810, a German scientist built a *heliograph* that sent "messages" (*graphs*) by directing "sunlight" (*helio*) to a specific place in the distance. During World War I (1914–1918), armies flashed messages from heliographs using Morse code, a code first used in 1844. The heliograph's main drawback is that it can only be used on sunny days.

A Royal Navy crewman sends a message on a heliograph in 1941.

Semaphores are another way to send messages over long distances. This device "carried" (*phore*) messages long distances by changing the position of two movable arms that each held a special "signal" (*sema*) flag. Each position of the arms and flags stood for a different letter or number. In the 1790s, Claude Chappe built semaphore stations atop hills in France. Men on each hill looked through telescopes at the semaphores on the two adjacent hills. Then

French officials test Chappe's semaphore system.

they passed the coded signal on to the next semaphore station. Messages could be sent about 130 miles (209 km) within a few minutes. Napoléon Bonaparte had a network of semaphore stations built throughout France because he recognized their value for national defense. The semaphore's drawback is that it can only be seen in daylight.

Bells and Smoke Signals in the Vatican

The Vatican is the pope's residence and the headquarters for the Roman Catholic Church. Traditional visual and sound signals are still used today to announce important events in the Vatican. For example, when a pope dies, a special bell is sounded. When the College of Cardinals does not reach a two-thirds vote for a new pope, the ballots are burned with wet straw so puffs of black smoke rise from a special chimney. When a two-thirds vote is reached and a new pope is elected, the ballots are burned with dry straw so puffs of white smoke are released from the chimney. And a bell is rung to announce the election.

Within Earshot

Although the human voice is carried only several yards through the air, louder sounds from horns, bells, drums, and sirens can travel farther. In biblical times, rams' horns were blown to warn people of a coming attack or invasion. Various kinds of horns have also announced the arrival of kings and other important people. Church bells have announced the times of worship, and school bells have called children to class. Bells have also been used to warn of emergency situations.

Many groups of African and South American people have used "talking drums" to send messages from village to village. Different beats and degrees of loudness are used as a code. When the drummers of one village heard the drums from the neighboring village, they passed the message on to yet another village. When the president of the Republic of Côte d'Ivoire died in 1993, in addition to radio and television reports, talking drums carried the news of his death throughout the country.

Today, sirens are commonly used as sound signals. Some of them warn of coming natural disasters, such as tornadoes or tsunamis. Emergency vehicles such as police cars, fire engines, and ambulances also use sirens. They warn other drivers to pull over and let them through.

Runners, Pigeons, and the Pony Express

Besides visual and sound signals carrying messages, people and animals have delivered messages across long distances. Sometimes runners or riders on horseback memorized the message, traveled a certain distance, and then passed the message on to another messenger. Unfortunately, when messages are relayed in this way, sometimes parts of the message are left out or the entire message gets mixed up.

When people started sending written messages, carrier pigeons were sometimes used to deliver them. Pigeons brought news about winners of the early Olympic Games to city-states throughout Greece. Messages were strapped to the pigeon's leg or placed in a small container attached

U.S. carrier pigeons were identified by numbers imprinted on their wings.

to its leg. During World War I (1914–1918), pigeons carried information across battlefields.

By the 1800s, most countries had some kind of postal system to deliver mail over long distances. In the United

States, mail was carried by stagecoaches and railroads. For eighteen months in 1860 and 1861, the Pony Express delivered mail between St. Joseph, Missouri, and Sacramento, California—about 2,000 miles (3,218 km). In good weather, Pony Express riders could cover that distance in about ten days. They would ride 100 miles (160 km), switching to a fresh horse every 10 miles (16 km), and then another rider would take over. The Pony Express was faster than stagecoaches, and the *transcontinental* railroad wouldn't link the eastern and western parts of the United States until 1869.

In October 1861, however, the transcontinental *telegraph* was completed. It linked the East Coast and the West Coast of the United States. The Pony Express was no longer necessary. Mail carried by galloping horses and speeding trains was soon replaced by electrical signals sent along wires.

Electricity: The Telegraph and Morse Code

During the late 1700s and early 1800s, several scientists in Europe and the United States experimented with electricity. Through those experiments, they learned several things. First, electricity moved quickly along wires. Second, electric current could be stored in a battery. Third, an electromagnet could be created by winding wire around an iron bar and attaching the wire to a battery. Fourth, clicking signals could be sent from one electromagnet to another.

There was one problem, however, that had to be solved. Electric current becomes weaker the farther it travels. As a result, the clicking signals sent from one electromagnet to another grow weaker, too.

To solve this problem, Joseph Henry (1797–1878), an American scientist and professor at the College of New Jersey (present-day Princeton University), designed a relay system. By placing batteries at equal spaces along the wire, the current remained strong and clicking signals could be sent along the entire length of the wire. In 1831, Henry was able to send a signal along 1 mile (1.6 km) of wire. This was the beginning of the telegraph—a new way to send written messages over long distances.

The Relay Principle

In a relay race, runners race around a track and then hand off a baton, or stick, to the next runner on their team. The baton must be handed off smoothly so the next runner can keep the race going. Bonfires, semaphores, talking drums, and the Pony Express also worked on the relay principle. They were successful methods of long-distance communication because they kept messages moving strongly from station to station or from rider to rider. Joseph Henry's electric relays kept a strong signal moving along the telegraph wire. Relays also play an important part in sending voice messages over long distances.

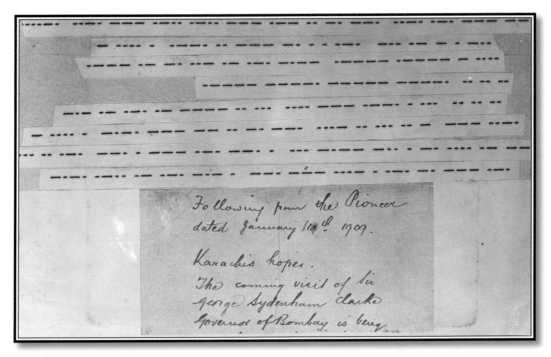

The first Morse code message from India arrived in London on January 10, 1909.

About the same time, Samuel F. B. Morse (1791–1872) became interested in the telegraph. He was a well-known artist but had done well in science courses at Yale College (present-day Yale University). By 1837, Morse had invented a code of dots and dashes that could be tapped out over a telegraph wire. Each combination of dots and dashes stood for a letter, a number, or a punctuation mark. He also invented an electromagnetic machine used to tap out a coded message. Each tap sent a pulse of electricity along the wire. At the other end of the wire in another telegraph machine, the electrical pulses were converted back to the dot and dash coded message.

Morse convinced the U.S. Congress to fund a telegraph line from Baltimore, Maryland, to Washington, D.C. The line was strung on poles next to the tracks of the Baltimore and Ohio Railroad. The first telegraph message was sent on May 1, 1844, from outside of Baltimore. It announced that Henry Clay had been nominated as a presidential candidate. A train carrying the same news arrived in Washington more than an hour later than the telegram. On May 24, 1844, the first official telegram was sent from the Supreme Court in Washington to the train station in Baltimore. Morse tapped out the famous message, "What hath God wrought!"

Newspapers soon used the telegraph to receive news stories from other cities and states. Businesses across the country sent and received telegraphed orders for goods. Ordinary people sent telegrams to family members with birth, wedding, and death announcements. Almost everyone thought the telegraph and telegrams would be the last inventions needed for long-distance communication. After all, the telegraph did fulfill most of the requirements of long-distance communications. It could send messages quickly over long distances. The messages were clearly understood. The sender of a telegram did have to wait for a reply, but for most people this wasn't a big problem. Within a few years, however, a boy who would come up with a solution to that problem and transform long-distance communication was born in Scotland.

CHAPTER THREE

Alexander Graham Bell

From a young age, Alexander Graham Bell was curious about the world around him. Aleck, as his family called him, enjoyed long walks, as well as sitting in a quiet spot to read and to think. During his walks, he picked up the kinds of things that appeal to most boys—shells, rocks, broken birds' eggs, and interesting plants. Later, Aleck wrote his observations in notebooks, one of

A photograph of Alexander Graham Bell at age fourteen

which he called his Thought Book. Observing, thinking, and writing down thoughts were good habits for a future inventor to develop.

The Bell Family

On March 3, 1847, in Edinburgh, Scotland, Alexander Graham Bell was born to Alexander Melville Bell (1819–1905) and Eliza Grace Symonds Bell (1809–1897). Little Aleck wasn't given his middle name at birth. He was just Alexander Bell, named after his grandfather Alexander

The Bell family relaxes in the garden at Milton Cottage near Edinburgh, Scotland. (from left, Melville James, Alexander Graham, Eliza Grace Symonds, Edward Charles, and Alexander Melville)

Bell (1790–1865). To distinguish between Aleck's father and grandfather, his father was called Melville. Aleck was the Bell's second son. His older brother, Melville James (1845–1870), was known as Melly, to distinguish between him and his father. Aleck's younger brother was Edward Charles (1848–1867).

Aleck was part of a well-educated and talented family. His grandfather was a stage actor who later taught speech and elocution. As an elocution teacher, Grandfather Bell taught actors and public speakers how to talk clearly and to project their voices to the back rows of an audience. This was an important skill at the time because microphones hadn't been invented yet. He also helped people with speech problems, such as stuttering and stammering.

Melville Bell, Aleck's father, was also a speech and elocution teacher. He held teaching positions at Edinburgh University, the University of London, and Queen's College in Ontario, Canada. Melville also wrote several textbooks on speech and speaking. He is best known for developing a system called Visible Speech. This was a code of symbols that showed the position of the throat, tongue, and lips for every possible sound that a person could make. The symbols could be applied to any language. After working on Visible Speech for almost twenty years, Melville's book, *Visible Speech: The Science of Universal Alphabetics*, was finally published in 1867.

The Bells on Broadway?

In 1912, the Anglo-Irish playwright George Bernard Shaw wrote *Pygmalion*. The play told how a speech professor, Henry Higgins, could teach anyone to speak proper English. In the preface to the play, Shaw acknowledges Alexander Melville Bell's work. That is why many people think that Shaw based the Higgins character on Alexander Melville Bell. The play was a great success. In the late 1950s, the Broadway musical *My Fair Lady* was adapted from Shaw's play. In the 1960s, the musical was made into a film.

Aleck's mother, Eliza, had also received a fine education. She excelled as an artist and pianist. By the time Melville and Eliza married in 1844, she was experiencing hearing loss. The only way she could hear was through an ear trumpet. With his family's background, it is not surprising that Aleck was interested in speech, sound, and deafness.

Bell's Early Years

Until he was ten years old, Aleck was taught at home by his mother. Besides the usual school subjects, Eliza also taught Aleck to play the piano. She would listen to him practice by putting the mouthpiece of her ear trumpet on the piano's soundboard. Aleck could play any tune by ear and easily learned to read music. He enjoyed playing the piano throughout his life. Aleck, however, showed little enthusiasm for regular school subjects, so his mother allowed him to follow his interests by exploring nature. The Bell's summer cottage outside of Edinburgh was the perfect place for exploring.

What's in a Name?

Aleck wanted to distinguish himself from the other Alexander Bells in the family. So on his eleventh birthday, he gave himself the middle name Graham. He took the name from Alexander Graham, one of his father's students from Canada. Aleck began signing his name A. Graham Bell, and his family started calling him Graham.

In 1858, both Aleck and Edward entered Edinburgh High School. By this time, Melly had already established himself as the scholar in the family. While Aleck did well in reading, speaking, and spelling, Melly consistently won awards for excellence. Edward's interest was in art, but his frail health worried the Bells more than his progress in school. High school was a six-year program. Melly was the only Bell son who graduated. Aleck left the school after four years of Latin, Greek, English, history, geography, basic science, and math.

In 1862, at age fifteen, Aleck went to London to spend a year with Grandfather Bell. His grandfather felt that Aleck was getting lost between Melly's awards and Edward's illnesses. Grandfather taught Aleck how to dress and act like a gentleman. He gave Aleck lessons in elocution and speaking. They read Shakespeare's plays together, and Grandfather pushed Aleck to read serious books on all subjects. Aleck began to enjoy studying and even thought about going to college.

At the end of the year, Melville went to London to pick up his son. Before they left, Melville and Aleck visited Sir Charles Wheatstone, a famous scientist. Wheatstone had done experiments with sound. He had built a speaking machine that was able to say a few simple words and sentences. Wheatstone demonstrated the machine for the Bells and gave them drawings and descriptions of the machine. Back in Edinburgh, Melville challenged Aleck and Melly to build a similar machine.

Bell Begins Work with Speech and Sound

Aleck and Melly did make a speaking machine. Aleck used gutta-percha, a rubbery material that hardens, to make a cast of teeth and jaws from a human skull. He used soft rubber for the lips. Aleck made a flexible wooden tongue by cutting the wood crosswise into sections, padding each section with cotton and covering the entire tongue with a piece of soft rubber. Each section of the tongue could be moved separately as a real person does when speaking. For the *hard palate,* or roof of the mouth, Aleck stuffed a piece of hard rubber with cotton. The boys used a tin tube for the throat and two pieces of rubber angled toward each other for the *vocal cords.* The vocal cords are in the larynx, and they vibrate and produce sounds when people speak.

The machine was also able to produce sound. When Melly blew into the throat and Aleck moved the lips, hard palate, and tongue, they got their machine to cry "Mama." Neighbors thought a real baby was crying.

In 1864, Melville had completed his book *Visible Speech*

Alexander Graham Bell instructs a student in Visible Speech.

and had taught his sons how the system worked. To gain a publisher for the book, he and the boys gave demonstrations of this system. With the boys in another room, audience members would make various vocal sounds, including words in foreign languages and animal or machine sounds. Melville would write the Visible Speech symbol for each sound on a blackboard. Then the boys would come

31

[ENGLISH ALPHABET OF VISIBLE SPEECH,
Expressed in the Names of Numbers and Objects.]

[Pronounce the Nos.]	[Names.]	[Name the Objects.]		[Name the Objects.]	
1.					
2.					
3.					
4.					
5.					
6.					
7.					
8.					

Each sound in the English language has a corresponding symbol in the Visible Speech system. This table shows the names of some objects and numbers in Visible Speech symbols.

into the room, look at the symbols, and make the correct sounds. Melville thought his system could help the deaf learn to speak. The symbols would show them the correct position of their tongue, lips, and mouth for each sound. When Aleck began working with the deaf, he used this system.

In 1866, Aleck began doing his own experiments with sound. Using two tuning forks, he realized that vowel sounds have two *pitches* rather than one. Pitch is the highness or lowness of a sound, such as the notes in the musical scale. Although German scientist Hermann von Helmholtz had already made that discovery, Aleck didn't know it at the time. Aleck later used this knowledge as he worked to invent a telegraph that could send several messages at once over one wire.

Bell As Teacher and Student

During the 1860s, Aleck and Melly took turns being teachers and students. In 1863, Aleck took his first teaching position at Weston House, while Melly went to Edinburgh University. Weston was a boys' boarding school in northern Scotland where Aleck taught music and speech in exchange for lessons in Greek and Latin. The following year, Aleck attended Edinburgh University, where he also studied Latin and Greek. In 1865, Aleck returned to Weston House and also taught part-time at a nearby girls' school.

In 1865, Grandfather Bell died, and Aleck's parents and Edward moved into his home in London. Two years later, Edward contracted tuberculosis, which was incurable at the time, and died. Aleck took on a teaching position at a school in England and was also preparing to receive a degree from University College in London. Then in 1870, Melly contracted tuberculosis and died. Aleck was suffering from headaches and having trouble sleeping. Because the Bells were afraid of losing Aleck, too, they decided to move to Canada for its a healthier climate. Melville had made trips to Canada and the United States, and he was well-known there because of his Visible Speech system.

Bell's Work with the Deaf

The Bells left England on July 21, 1870, and arrived in Canada on August 1. They bought a house and settled in Brantford, Ontario. Melville had been offered a teaching position at the Boston School for Deaf Mutes, where he would use his Visible Speech system. A mute person is

Bell used the Visible Speech system in his work with deaf students at the Boston School for Deaf Mutes.

someone who cannot talk. Melville didn't want to teach his own system, but he thought Aleck would be perfect for the job. In April 1871, using Visible Speech, Aleck began teaching thirty deaf children how to talk. He also instructed the other teachers in how to use the Visible Speech system. His students showed such progress in a short amount of time that he was offered positions at other schools for the deaf, including the Clarke Institution for Deaf Mutes. Then in 1873, Aleck became a professor of Vocal Physiology and Elocution at Boston University. Vocal physiology is the study of how the mouth, lips, throat, and larynx work.

In addition to his teaching positions, Aleck also tutored students privately. In 1872, Thomas Sanders gave Aleck room and board in exchange for tutoring his four-year-old son George, who had been born deaf. Within two years, George could read and was beginning to speak. Aleck had written the letters of the alphabet on a glove. Using the glove, George could "talk" to people by spelling out words. In 1873, Mabel Hubbard (1857–1923) became another pupil. She had lost her hearing at age five after having scarlet fever. Although she could still speak, she was sometimes hard to understand. Mabel's father was Gardiner Greene Hubbard, a patent attorney and president of the Clarke Institution for Deaf Mutes. He was also interested in finding a way to send several messages at once over one telegraph wire.

Bell Starts Thinking Like an Inventor

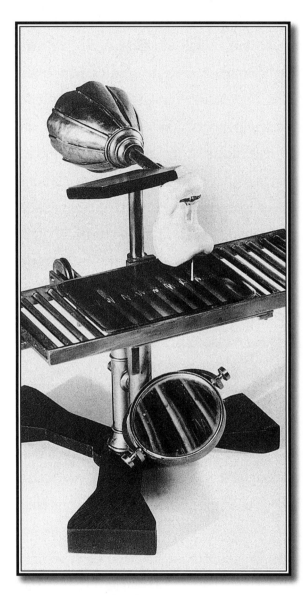

Bell invented the phonautograph in 1874 to create visual images of sounds. He hoped the machine would help deaf people "see" speech.

When Bell wasn't teaching or tutoring, he attended public lectures on scientific subjects, such as electricity. In this way, he met and got to know the leading scientists and thinkers of the time. Bell also tinkered with ways to send sound over a wire and ways to help the deaf "see" sound.

In the summer of 1874, at his parents' home in Canada, Bell made a device called a *phonautograph,* which he hoped would help the deaf see speech. This machine was made up of a speaking tube that was attached to a human ear (a dead man's ear given to Bell by a doctor) that in turn was attached to a piece of straw that moved over a flat piece of smoked glass. When Bell spoke into the tube, the sound passed from the outer ear and caused the eardrum to vibrate, which in turn caused the bones in the inner ear to vibrate, thus causing the straw to move back and forth and make wavy lines on the smoked glass. These lines were images of sound waves from the human voice.

One day, after working with the phonautograph, Bell went to his "dreaming place"—a spot that overlooked the river near his parents' home. It was there that Bell began to think that if sound waves from the human voice could cause a piece of straw to move and reproduce the waves of the human voice, perhaps the human voice could be sent over a wire, just like a telegram.

At the end of the summer, Bell was ready to return to Boston and his students, especially Mabel Hubbard. Bell was ten years older than Mabel. As they got to know each other during their many tutoring sessions, they fell in love. They became engaged in 1875 but did not marry until Bell had a good income. This occurred in 1877, a year after he had invented the telephone and shortly after he, Sanders, Hubbard, and Thomas Watson had founded the Bell Telephone Company. Aleck and Mabel enjoyed a long and happy marriage. They had two daughters, Elsie and Marian (Daisy), and two sons who died shortly after birth.

Helen Keller (1880–1968)

No story about Alexander Graham Bell would be complete without mentioning Helen Keller (left). When she was only nineteen months old, Helen was struck with an undiagnosed illness that left her blind and deaf. Because she couldn't hear, she lost the ability to speak. When she was six years old, one of Helen's doctors suggested that her father contact Bell to locate a teacher for her. Bell recommended that Arthur Keller contact the Perkins Institution for the Blind. That school sent Annie Sullivan (right) to be Helen's teacher. Sullivan taught Helen how to communicate with the manual alphabet. A few years later, Helen demanded to learn how to speak and was sent to the Horace Mann School for the Deaf in Boston.

Over the years, Helen spent much time with the Bell family and became great friends with Bell's daughters, who were only a few years older than she. In 1904, she amazed the country by graduating with honors from Radcliffe College. Helen went on to write several books, including her autobiography, *The Story of My Life*, which was dedicated to Alexander Graham Bell. She spent the rest of her life giving talks to raise money for the education of the blind.

CHAPTER FOUR

"Mr. Watson— Come Here— I Want to See You"

Bell's experiences making the speaking machine, teaching Visible Speech, experimenting with the pitch of vowels, and using the phonautograph helped lead him to the invention of the telephone. Although his main interest was helping the deaf learn to speak, he also was caught up with the excitement of new electrical inventions. In the 1870s, Boston, Massachusetts, was the center of this activity. There the Charles Williams Machine Shop attracted inventors who were working on electrical machines. The shop produced electrical equipment for telegraphs and fire alarms. Williams' machinists also built batteries, call bells for hotels, and equipment for school science labs. In addition, Williams provided a laboratory in the attic for inventors working on electrical machines.

The main machine many inventors, including Bell, were trying to perfect was the multiple telegraph.

Forming a Partnership

From the time that Bell realized that vowels have two pitches, he thought that several messages could be sent at once over a single telegraph wire by varying the pitch of each message. At the receiving end of the telegram, tuning forks of varying pitches would sort out the signals for each message. By the early 1870s, Thomas Edison had invented a way to send up to four messages at a time over

Thomas Watson (right) was a talented young machinist who agreed to work with Bell in 1875.

a single telegraph wire. This still wasn't enough because so many people were sending telegrams. Bell thought it was possible to send as many as thirty or forty messages at a time. This would help the telegraph companies serve more customers. At the same time, it would save the telegraph companies from having to install more telegraph poles and string more wires.

In the fall of 1874, Thomas Sanders and Gardiner Hubbard agreed to financially support Bell's experiments in return for a share in any profits that a *patent* on the harmonic telegraph might bring. Bell called his machine the harmonic telegraph because it was based on different levels of pitch or musical notes.

Bell had the basic ideas and could build simple equipment. He was clumsy, however, when it came to working with the small parts needed for the more complicated equipment that was used to create the harmonic telegraph. Luckily, Bell met Thomas Watson, a young, creative machinist at the Charles Williams Machine Shop. In January 1875, Watson agreed to work with Bell in the evenings. The two men became good friends as they worked many late nights in the attic of the machine shop.

From Harmonic Telegraph to the Telephone

In February 1875, Bell took the harmonic telegraph to Washington, D.C. He demonstrated it to William Orton, president of Western Union, the largest telegraph company. The machine didn't use tuning forks. Instead, it used metal reeds of different lengths to send and receive messages of different pitches. Bell had also added thirty styluses that would record Morse code dots and dashes to a strip of moving paper at the telegraph's receiver. Bell intended to apply for a patent for this telegraph. Two days before Bell arrived in Washington, Elisha Gray had applied for a patent for a similar telegraph. Unlike Bell's telegraph, however, Gray's telegraph did not have a way to record the dots and dashes. Bell was granted a patent for that part of his invention.

U.S. Patents

The U.S. Constitution gives Congress the power to grant patents. To carry out this function, Congress set up the U.S. Patent and Trademark Office. A patent is a written document that assures an inventor the exclusive right to make, use, and sell an invention for a certain period of time. The first patent was issued in 1790 to Samuel Hopkins for inventing a new way of manufacturing potash. During the years between that first patent and Bell's patent, about 175,000 patents were issued. Since then, about 6 million patents have been issued. In 2004 alone, 187,170 were issued—and of those, about 10,500 were for improvements to telephone equipment and systems.

While Bell was in Washington, he visited Joseph Henry, who had been appointed as the first director of the Smithsonian Institution in 1846. Henry was a pioneer in the use of electricity, having built the first electric motor and the first telegraph. Bell sought Henry's advice about the harmonic telegraph. Bell also shared his thoughts about sending the human voice over wires—in other words, building a telephone. Henry urged Bell to drop his work on the harmonic telegraph and to refine his ideas for the telephone. Bell felt that he didn't have enough knowledge of electricity. Henry said, "Get it!"

Because Hubbard and Sanders were backing him to build the harmonic telegraph, Bell continued to perfect it. Sometimes reeds would slip out of place. Other times

Physicist Joseph Henry was born in 1797. He became the first director of the Smithsonian Institution in 1846.

sparking would occur. Bell began to spend more time thinking about how he might build a telephone.

Bell and Watson had set up the telegraph's *transmitter* in the attic of the machine shop and its *receiver* on the second floor. A wire connected the two ends. On the hot afternoon of June 2, 1875, Bell had a breakthrough. He and Watson were tuning the reeds on the telegraph's transmitter and receiver. Watson had overtightened a screw on one of the reeds, so electric current was continually running through it. When Watson plucked that reed on his transmitter, Bell heard the sound on his receiver. Bell had Watson do it again, and the same thing happened. Bell then realized that the vibration of the sound waves created on Watson's reed was carried through the wire and transmitted to the reed on his transmitter. Bell also realized that the only way to send the human voice over wire was with a continuous current, not the intermittent current needed to send dots and dashes.

Developments Happen Quickly and Then Stop

For all practical purposes, Bell and Watson stopped working on the telegraph and put their energies into developing the telephone. Bell combined his knowledge of how the human voice and human ear worked with his new knowledge of how electricity worked. Bell would sketch out how he thought the telephone might work, and

44

Watson would build a device. First, Watson devised a thin leather *diaphragm,* similar to the eardrum. A diaphragm is a thin, flexible disk that vibrates when sound waves hit it, such as in a telephone's mouthpiece, or that vibrates to create sound, such as in a telephone's receiver. This first diaphragm was too thin. It broke when spoken into, and the sound was faint on the other end.

On July 1, 1875, Watson made a thicker diaphragm for the transmitter. This time, when Bell spoke into the transmitter, Watson could hear sounds but not words from the receiver. When Bell sang into the transmitter, Watson could hear a tune, but again no words. Then Watson made a diaphragm for the receiver. When Bell sang and talked into it, Watson could hear his voice but could not make out the words. Bell was sure that the telephone would work with just a bit more tinkering. Hubbard, however, insisted Bell return to work on the telegraph. Then Watson got sick, and Bell returned to Canada for the rest of the summer. Experiments with the telephone would have to wait for a few months.

Patent Number 174,465

With the beginning of a new school year, Bell returned to teaching at Boston University by day and working on the telephone at night. He also was writing the application for a patent on his invention. His application was so clearly and carefully worded that it would later stand up to more than 600 challenges by other would-be inventors of the telephone. First, he explained the theory of using a vibrating or wavelike current of electricity. Second, he stated the way the electrical vibrations would be produced within the telephone. Third, he proposed that one use of the electrical vibrations would be to transmit vocal sounds telegraphically.

On February 14, 1876, Hubbard submitted the patent for Bell. Two hours later on that same day, Elisha

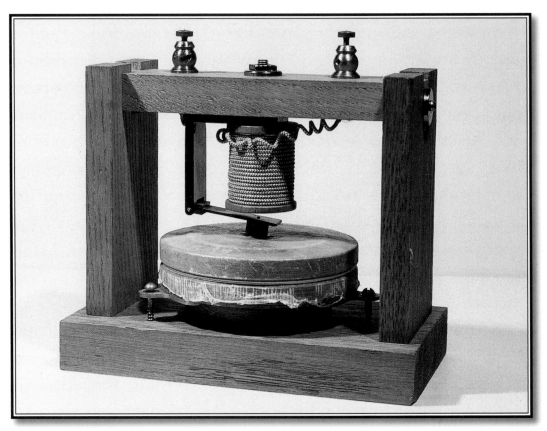

A model of the Bell's first telephone

Gray filed a caveat, or announcement, that he planned to submit a patent for a telephone. On March 3, 1876, Bell's twenty-ninth birthday, he was granted U.S. Patent Number 174,465. This is said to be the most valuable patent ever issued. Bell would become a millionaire from the profits generated by the telephone.

The Invention of the Telephone

At this point, however, the telephone had yet to be invented. On March 8, Bell and Watson resumed their experiments in rooms that Bell had rented in a private home. The transmitter was in Bell's study, and the receiver was across the hall in his bedroom. Bell's earlier experiments had used an electromagnet in the transmitter. This time, he substituted a small cup of water for the electromagnet. He wound wire around a tuning fork and connected the wire to the receiver and then to a battery. The other end of the wire was placed in the cup. The arms of the tuning fork were placed partially in the water. When Bell struck the tuning fork, a faint sound was heard at the receiver. By adding acid to the water, the sound became louder. Bell concluded that if the vibrating object touched only a small area of the water, it would vibrate more and produce a louder sound.

On March 9, Bell had Watson build a box with a diaphragm as the bottom. From the diaphragm hung an ordinary sewing needle, whose tip just touched the acid water. When Bell sang into the box, the different pitches of the song were heard at the receiver. Then Watson talked into the box, and mumbling sounds were heard from the receiver.

On March 10, Watson attached a brass pipe to the wire in the acid water and replaced the ordinary needle with a platinum one. Watson also made a hornlike mouthpiece that replaced the box. Then Watson went across the hall into Bell's bedroom and waited. The doors between the two rooms were closed. Bell then spoke into the mouthpiece, "Mr. Watson—come here—I want to see you." Watson heard this sentence, ran into the other room, and repeated what Bell had said. For the rest of the evening,

Bell's telephone was a big attraction at the American Centennial Exhibition in Philadelphia in June 1876. This is a replica of the telephone transmitter he exhibited there.

they took turns speaking into the telephone. During the next few months, Bell continued to refine the invention. He finally went back to using electromagnets rather than acid water to transmit the sound. This became known as the magneto telephone.

Thomas Watson (1854–1934)

Though he had little formal education, Thomas Watson was a mechanical and electrical genius. He could quickly figure out the fastest and best way to complete a task. Watson was born in Salem, Massachusetts, a town near Boston. A restless boy, he left school at the age of fourteen. He had several jobs before he started work at the Charles Williams Machine Shop in 1872. While there, he developed new tools that improved his work. He also studied scientific principles that could be used in his work.

Because of the work he did with Bell in inventing the telephone, Watson became one of the partners in the Bell Telephone Company. He remained with the company until 1881. In 1884, he formed a partnership for a ship and engine building company that built warships for the U.S. government. Watson retired in 1904 and spent the rest of his life traveling and studying literature, music, and painting. He even acted in Shakespearean plays in England. In 1926, his autobiography, *Exploring Life*, was published. In it, he mentions that Bell had spilled acid on his pants and that's why he said, "Mr. Watson—come here—I want to see you." Historians think that Watson added this bit to make the invention of the telephone a more dramatic story.

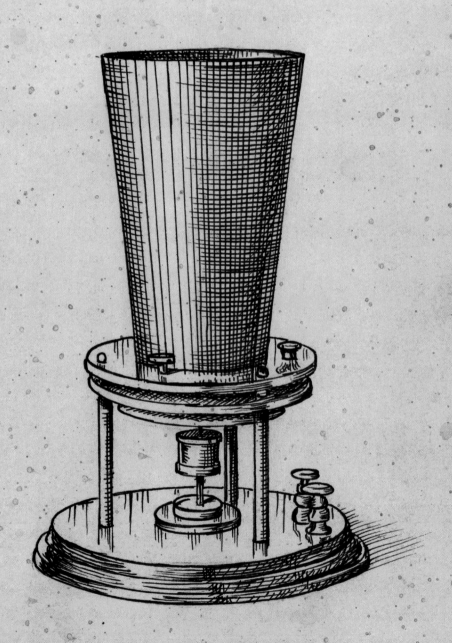

Creating a Demand for the Telephone

On June 25, 1876, Bell gave the first public demonstration of the telephone at the Centennial Exposition in Philadelphia. This fair was held to celebrate the one hundredth birthday of the United States. Dom Pedro, the emperor of Brazil, and several famous scientists judged the electrical inventions that had been entered at the fair. When Dom Pedro heard Bell's voice come out of the receiver, he exclaimed, "I hear! I hear!" The other judges took turns listening. They couldn't talk to Bell because the receiver could not transmit. They awarded Bell the gold medal for his invention.

On October 6, Bell and Watson had the first two-way phone conversation. Bell had discovered that the diaphragm transmitter also worked as a receiver. On October 9, they had the first long-distance call. This took place between Boston and Cambridge over a 2-mile (3.2 km) telegraph line. The two men continued to perfect the telephone. On January 30, 1877, Bell was issued his second telephone patent, which included the use of a metal diaphragm and electromagnet.

In 1877, Bell and Watson gave public demonstrations of the telephone to large audiences. The most famous of these demonstrations took place on February 12. Bell was in an auditorium in Salem, Massachusetts, and Watson was in Bell's room in Boston. Watson said, "Hoy!

Bell and Watson demonstrated the telephone in front of large audiences such as this one in Salem, Massachusetts.

Hoy!" Bell responded with, "Hoy! Hoy!" Then Watson sang "Yankee Doodle" and "Auld Lang Syne" and read newspaper articles. The audiences loved it, and orders for telephones poured in. By June 1877, more than 230 telephones had been installed in homes and businesses in and around Boston. The Bell Telephone Company was officially founded on July 9, with Bell, Watson, Hubbard, and Sanders as partners. Over time, the company grew and became American Telephone and Telegraph (AT&T).

"Hoy! Hoy!" or "Hello"

During the first few years of the telephone's existence, there was a debate over the proper way to answer the phone. Bell preferred "Hoy! Hoy!" and used it throughout his life. Thomas Edison, another great inventor who made improvements to the telephone, preferred the simpler and less dramatic, "Hello."

A True Inventor

Bell continued to experiment with the telephone. In 1880, he successfully transmitted the human voice over a ray of light with a photophone. This is similar to the way calls are now transmitted over fiber optic cables. He also predicted that, in time, people would be able to merely push a button and make a call without using an operator. In 1892, with Bell in New York and Hubbard in Chicago, Bell took part in the first long-distance call between those cities. This was the only time he was photographed using his invention. In 1915, Bell was in New York and talked for twenty-three minutes to his old friend Watson in San Francisco. This was the first transcontinental telephone call.

In 1879, Bell invented the audiometer, which measures hearing ability. For this reason, the decibel was named for him. This is the unit of measurement for the loudness of sounds. By 1880, Bell and his wife, Mabel, had settled in Washington, D.C. There he resumed his work teaching and helping the deaf. In 1885, the Bells started building a huge summer home called Beinn Bhreagh ("beautiful mountains") on the sea in Nova Scotia. There Bell would work on new inventions, including flying machines (1891–1909) and hydrofoil boats (1911). On August 2, 1922, Bell died at Beinn Bhreagh. On the day of his burial, all AT&T phones in North America were silent for one minute.

Totally Connected

After Alexander Graham Bell spoke the sentence, "Mr. Watson—come here—I want to see you," and Thomas Watson heard it over that first telephone, the world changed forever. Thomas Edison said that Bell had shrunk time and space and had brought the human family closer together. By connecting people anywhere in the world in an instant, the telephone definitely makes it easy to stay in touch. Indeed, the telephone has had a great impact on all aspects of life—social, economic, political, and cultural.

The Good, the Bad, and the Annoying

The telephone makes it possible for anyone with a phone to make or receive a call to or from anyone else with a phone. The good thing about this is that people can call for help in an emergency. Some of the first telephone calls were placed through an operator to a doctor, the police, or a fire station. Today, almost every town has 911 service for crime, fire, or health emergencies. About 165 million 911 calls are made each year. About 50 million of them are from cell phones. There are many other special help lines. Some are crisis lines for people suffering from mental illnesses. They can call and get advice or help from a counselor. There are even turkey help lines, which bewildered cooks can call to get help preparing the big bird for Thanksgiving dinner.

A few people use the phone to make prank or crank calls. Some of these calls are obscene or threatening. It is against the law to use the phone to make such calls. Now that many people have caller identification on their phones, the number of crank calls has gone down. Crank callers don't want to be caught.

Workers answer emergency calls at a 911 call center in Los Angeles, California.

Other phone calls are just plain annoying. Every day, telemarketers make thousands of sales calls over the phone. They try to sell everything from new windows to new long-distance service. Many other callers take surveys or polls over the phone.

In 2003, the U.S. government established the National Do-Not-Call Registry. Anyone can register their phone numbers by going to this Web site: http://www.donotcall.gov.

The Telephone and the Environment

To supply the need for telephone poles in the late 1800s, more than 45,000 of Vermont's pine trees were cut down. As telephone lines expanded across the country, more forests were cut down. To connect transcontinental telephone service, more than 14,000 miles (22,531 km) of wire were strung from 130,000 poles. As more homes and businesses received phone service, cities and towns became a maze of wires. People complained about how ugly the wires looked. By the 1890s, telephone wires in many cities were buried underground.

Today, cell phone towers receive the same complaints. To get around the objections, some cell phone companies disguise the towers. In California and Florida, they are shaped to look like palm trees. In other places, they are hidden in church steeples or attached to streetlights and chimneys. In rural areas, they are disguised as grain silos.

The Telephone's Effect on the Economy

Telecommunications makes up one of the largest industries in the United States and throughout the world. This industry includes wired phones, cordless phones, cell phones, fax services, and the Internet. In the United States, more than one million people are employed in this industry. About 25 percent of them work for wireless, or cell phone, companies. Telecommunications workers make phones, sell phones and phone services, string lines for new phone connections, build cell phone towers, repair connections, design new and better phones, and develop faster ways to send phone calls.

In the United States, there are 116 telephone numbers for every 100 people. This means that many people have more that one *telephone line* or cell phone number. About 97 percent of U.S. homes have phone service with at least one telephone line. No business can survive without at least two telephone lines and additional lines for fax machines and Internet connections. Throughout the world, however, only 40 percent of the people have any kind of phone service. Many of them rely on using pay phones to place calls. Worldwide, telecommunications services generate more than $1 trillion in U.S. currency. That includes wired telephone, cell phone, fax, and Internet connections.

Government and the Telephone

In 1879, President Rutherford Hayes had the first telephone installed in the White House. President Herbert Hoover (1929–1933) was the first president to have a phone on his desk in the Oval Office. By that time, there were three phones in the White House. The other phones were in an outer office and in the president's living quarters. The most famous White House phone service is known as the "hotline" or the "red phone." The phones aren't red, however; they are a pale yellow. Set up in 1963, the line directly connects the U.S. president and the leader of Russia. All either one has to do is lift the receiver and they're automatically connected, with no dialing needed. Leaders of the two countries have used the hotline many times during world crises.

Until 1934, the U.S. government did not regulate the telephone system. That changed when Congress established the Federal Communications Commission (FCC). The members of this group regulate all communication systems (radio, television, wire, satellite, and cable) within the United States and between the United States and other countries. Currently, the FCC ensures that all telephone and cellular companies operate fairly and that there is competition among long-distance phone services. The FCC also has programs that help low-income families receive discounts on telephone service.

Women, the Telephone, and Advertising

The first telephone operators were young men who had worked delivering telegraphs. Many of them were rude to the customers. As a result, telephone companies began hiring young women instead. The women had to be of good character and had to follow strict codes for dress and behavior on the job. Their voices had to be low, pleasant, and carry well. They could only say two things to customers: "Number, please;" and "Thank you." If an operator got married, she had to quit her job. Even under these conditions, thousands of women became switchboard operators. At that time, women had few employment opportunities other than teaching, nursing, or being a sales clerk in a store. In 1910, the New York Telephone Company alone employed 6,000 women at their switchboards. Today, thousands of women still work for telephone companies. Their jobs vary from designing better switchboards to installing telephone equipment.

Women were also pictured using telephones in advertisements. Early ads showed how women could order everything they needed over the phone—from groceries to clothing and furniture. Today's ads also prominently feature women. The phone is often portrayed as a tool to help organize a woman's life—from making appointments to organizing carpools.

Some of the first decorative phones were meant to stand out like a pretty lamp or vase. In 1959, the Princess phone was introduced as an *extension phone* for a young girl's room. The Trimline phone in 1965 was pitched to women as smaller and easier to hold. Today, cell phone ads appeal to everyone. The ads featuring family plans, however, are often geared to appeal to women as a way of keeping the whole family connected.

60

CHAPTER SIX

Continuing Development of Telephones and Telephone Service

You have grown up in the age of the cell phone, e-mail, and the Internet's World Wide Web (www). When your parents were young, faxes and answering machines were first becoming available to the general public. Your grandparents might remember the first colored phones and the first touch-tone phones. All of these changes in the ways people communicate evolved from the telephone that was invented in 1876. Technology continues to improve the functions of the telephone and the ways phone calls are sent and received.

The World's Largest Company

At first, Bell, Hubbard, and Sanders weren't sure they wanted to be in the telephone business. During the winter of 1876–1877, they offered to sell the telephone patent to Western Union for $100,000. Western Union was the main telegraph company, with wires strung across the country. That put the company in a good position to offer telephone service over those same wires. William Orton, the president of Western Union, turned the offer down. This is regarded as the worst business decision in history. As a result, Bell, Hubbard, Sanders, and Watson established the Bell Telephone Company in July 1877. The first Bell phones were made in the Charles Williams Machine Shop. In 1878, the four partners sold the company, which then became the American Bell Telephone Company.

In the meantime, Western Union had set up a new company, Western Electric, to make its own phones. After losing several court fights over patent rights, Western Union sold Western Electric to American Bell in 1881. In 1883, American Bell set up a separate company to work on ways to improve the telephone and the ways telephone service was delivered. This company became Bell Laboratories. In 1885, American Bell set up another company for long-distance service—the American Telephone and Telegraph Company (AT&T). In 1899, AT&T became the parent company of Western Electric, Bell Laboratories, and several Bell telephone companies throughout the country that supplied local phone services. In 1910, American Bell also gained control of Western Union, which remained a separate company.

AT&T used this image of a telephone in space with its cord wrapped around the world in its advertising campaigns during the 1940s.

By 1939, AT&T controlled 98 percent of long-distance service and 83 percent of local service in the United States. It also made 90 percent of all phone equipment sold in the United States. AT&T was considered a *monopoly.* It had almost complete control of the telephone industry. By the 1970s, AT&T was the world's largest company. In 1974, the U.S. government began the legal process to break up AT&T's monopoly. The breakup took effect in 1984. AT&T remained a long-distance service provider and kept Western Electric and Bell Laboratories. The local Bell phone companies were divided into seven separate regional companies with no connection to AT&T. In 1996, AT&T combined Western Electric and Bell Labs into a new company—Lucent Technologies.

After 1984, several new companies, such as MCI and Sprint, entered the long-distance telephone business. The Communications Act of 1996, passed by Congress, encouraged even more competition in the telephone business. The long-distance companies also began offering local service, and local phone companies began offering long-distance service. Every year since 1996, more independent phone companies have been founded. All of these companies, however, offer their services over lines maintained by AT&T. If you talked over a regular telephone, a cell phone, or used the Internet today, chances are that your message was transmitted over the national network AT&T designed, engineered, and built over the past three decades.

Changes in Telephone Service

The first telephone lines were direct wire connections between a home and a business, between two homes, or between two businesses. For example, the first telephone line connected Charles Williams's home and his machine shop in April 1877. The phones were boxes with a small opening to speak into and listen from. There was no dial tone or way to hang up. These phones were always on. To start a call, the person at one end just had to get the attention of the person at the other end.

In 1878, the first switchboard at a central exchange was used in New Haven, Connecticut. Home and business phone lines were then connected at the central exchange. When people wanted to place a call, they would push a button or turn a crank on their phone to connect to the central switchboard. A telephone operator would make the connection, and the other person's phone would ring. At

Telephone operators work at a switchboard in New York City in 1901.

first, each caller's phone line was identified on the switchboard with his or her name. In fact, the first telephone book (1878) was a one-page list of fifty names of individuals or businesses with phones in New Haven. Noted American author Samuel Clemens, better known as Mark Twain, was one of the residential telephone customers served by this switchboard. Eventually, phone lines were assigned numbers, which are now called telephone numbers.

The next big change occurred in 1889 when Almon Brown Strowger perfected the dial telephone and the automatic switchboard. Where this equipment was used, operators were no longer needed to connect local calls, but they still had to connect long-distance calls. In the 1960s, direct dialing finally replaced the operator for long-distance calls.

The Telephone in Songs, Movies, and Television

From the early 1900s, the telephone has played a role in songs, movies, television shows, and comedy routines. In the Broadway show *Havana*, the song "Cupid's Telephone" instructs a young man that if he hopes to win the love of a certain young woman, he should call her on the telephone. In 1915, the most popular song was "Hello Frisco." It was written after Bell and Watson made the first transcontinental phone call between New York and San Francisco. The Broadway musical and movie versions of *Bye-Bye Birdie* featured the song "The Telephone Hour." In the scene, several pairs of teenagers call each other to gossip and make plans for the weekend.

In some suspenseful mystery movies, the telephone seems to be the main character. *Dial M for Murder*, *Call Northside 777*, *Sorry Wrong Number*, and *Cellular* are a few of those movies. In the 1960s, *Get Smart* was a television comedy spy show. Maxwell Smart, the main character, had a secret phone in his shoe. Bob Newhart, a well-known actor and entertainer, became famous for his low-key comedy routines in which he pretended to talk on the phone.

Faxes, E-mail, and the Internet

The telephone was invented so that the human voice could be sent by electricity through wires. Today, data can also be sent through a telephone line. Data are the text messages and visuals that you send in e-mails. The first e-mail was sent in 1971. Data are also the pages of information that you see when you use the Internet.

Fax is short for facsimile, which means "exact copy." It wasn't until the 1980s that sending faxes of pictures or text could easily be done. A fax machine is really a photocopier with a telephone. First, the fax number of the recipient is dialed. Then the pages of paper with pictures or text are inserted into and copied by the machine, which breaks down the text or picture into a digital code. The code is carried through the phone line to the recipient's fax machine, which then reads the code, reconstructs the text or picture, and prints out an exact copy of the original pages.

The same thing happens when e-mail messages are sent from a computer through a modem to the telephone line: the message is turned into a digital code and reformatted through the modem at the other end. When someone connects to the Internet, his or her computer's modem dials up the Internet connection. The Internet user then receives text and visual information through the telephone line that is connected to the computer by a modem.

The Future Is Now

Most phone calls, e-mails, and Internet information are no longer transmitted over metal wires by electricity. Now, most of them are sent through fiber optic cable, which was developed in 1970. In fiber optic cables, thin, hairlike strands of glass carry voice and data messages via pulses of laser light. With fiber optics, messages are sent

From Wall Phones to Cell Phones

From 1877 to the present, designers have continually changed the size, shape, color, functions, and material of the phone.

1877–1880: Wall phones are made of oak or walnut wood; some have a combination transmitter-receiver, others have a separate transmitter and receiver.

1897: A desk-set phone made of brass becomes popular.

1920s: Desk-set phones are made of Bakelite—similar to a hard plastic—with dials.

1930s–1950s: Several changes take place in the style of desk–set phones.

1945: The mobile (cell) phone is invented.

1954: The first colored phones are offered in white, beige, green, pink, and blue.

1956: Wall phones are used in kitchens, basements, and garages.

1958: Speakerphones are introduced.

1964: Touch-tone phones make calling easier and faster.

1965: Trimline phones with a lighted dial take up less space.

1980s: Cordless phones are introduced; call waiting, call forwarding, and conference calling can be added as phone services.

1990s: Cell phones are made small enough to carry in a pocket or purse; caller ID is added as a phone service.

2000–present: More features are built into cell phones, including cameras, games, voice mail and the ability to send messages.

more quickly and clearly. Cell phones don't use any wires at all. Their voice and text messages are transmitted by radio waves that are sent out from cell phone towers. In addition, since 1962, communication satellites orbiting in space use radio waves to receive and send telephone calls from one country to another.

Changes to and improvements on the telephone and telephone delivery services are never ending. Almost every day, there is news about new telephone companies, mergers of existing ones, new features for telephones, or new uses for telephones. One of the latest developments is sending voice messages over the Internet. This is known as VoIP. Alexander Graham Bell probably couldn't have imagined all of the devices that would develop from his basic telephone, but they wouldn't have surprised him. After all, he did send a voice message on light waves in 1880.

The Telephone: A Timeline

The Bell Telephone Company is formed.
p. 50–51
The first telephone line is connected to a private home.
p. 64

Bell and Gardiner Hubbard take part in the first long-distance call between New York and Chicago. p. 51

Alexander Graham Bell is born.
p. 26

President Rutherford B. Hayes has the first telephone installed in the White House.
p. 57

The first coast-to-coast long-distance call is made between Bell in New York City and Thomas Watson in San Francisco.
p. 52

1847   1876   1877   1878   1879   1880   1892   1915   1922   1929

On March 3, Bell is granted a patent for the harmonic telegraph. On March 10, Bell invents the telephone in Boston, Massachusetts. p. 48

Bell sends the first voice message on light waves.
p. 51

Herbert Hoover is the first president to have a telephone on his desk in the Oval Office. p. 57

The first telephone switchboard exchange is set up in New Haven, Connecticut.
p. 64

Alexander Graham Bell dies.
p. 52

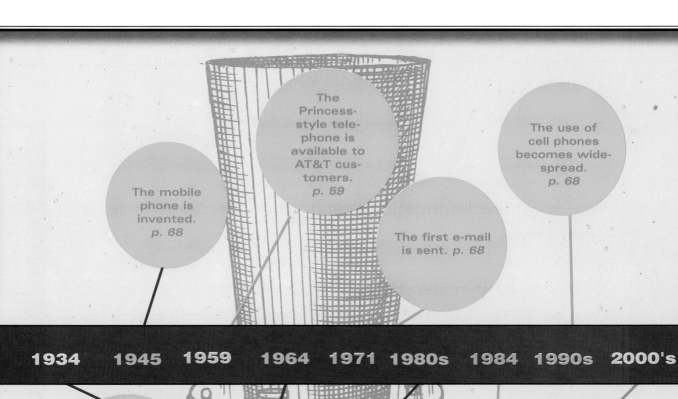

The mobile phone is invented. *p. 68*

The Princess-style telephone is available to AT&T customers. *p. 59*

The first e-mail is sent. *p. 68*

The use of cell phones becomes widespread. *p. 68*

1934   1945   1959   1964   1971   1980s   1984   1990s   2000's

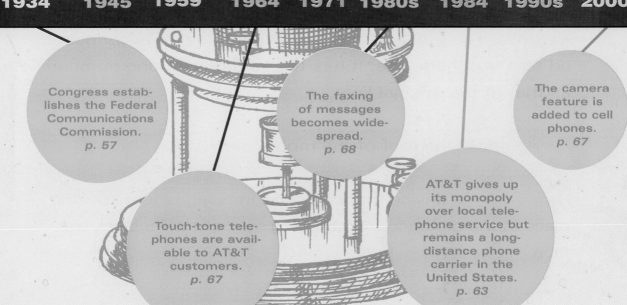

Congress establishes the Federal Communications Commission. *p. 57*

Touch-tone telephones are available to AT&T customers. *p. 67*

The faxing of messages becomes widespread. *p. 68*

AT&T gives up its monopoly over local telephone service but remains a long-distance phone carrier in the United States. *p. 63*

The camera feature is added to cell phones. *p. 67*

71

Glossary

communicate: to send and receive messages from others; to share information, ideas, thoughts, and feelings with others

diaphragm: thin, flexible disk that vibrates when sound waves hit it, such as in a telephone's mouthpiece, or vibrates to create sound, such as in a telephone's receiver

extension phone: an additional telephone that is connected to a telephone line; it has the same telephone number as that of the original line

hard palate: the roof of the mouth

heliograph: a device that can send messages to a specific place in the distance by reflecting sunlight off a shiny surface *monopoly:* complete control of a product or service

patent: a written document that assures an inventor of the exclusive right to make, use, and sell an invention for a certain period of time

phonautograph: a device that could reproduce the sound waves of the human voice on smoked glass

pitch: the highness or lowness of a sound, as in the notes of the musical scale

receiver: the earpiece or part of the telephone from which we hear another person's voice

semaphore: a system of sending visual signals by changing the position of movable arms and the position of the patterned flags that they hold

telecommunication: sending messages or signals over a distance

telegraph: a machine used to send coded messages of dots and dashes *telephone line:* the line or wire that connects a home or business to a local phone service; each line is assigned a separate telephone number

transcontinental: across a continent

transmitter: device to send signals over a wire or by radio waves

vocal cords: two flaps in the larynx that vibrate and produce sound when people speak

To Find Out More

Books

Holland, Gini, and Amy Stone. *Telephones.* New York: Marshall Cavendish, 1996.

McCormick, Anita Louise. *The Invention of the Telegraph and Telephone in American History.* Berkeley Heights, N.J.: Enslow Publishers, Inc., 2004.

Reid, Struan. *Alexander Graham Bell.* Chicago: Heinemann Library, 2001.

Sherman, Josepha. *The History of the Internet.* Danbury, Conn.: Franklin Watts, 2003.

St. George, Judith. *Dear Dr. Bell . . . Your Friend, Helen Keller.* New York: G.P. Putnam's Sons, 1992.

Video

The Telephone: The Invention That Forever Changed the Way We Communicate. The American Experience. A 60-minute PBS video narrated by Morley Safer, 1997.

Web Sites

Telecommunications History Group

http://telcomhistory.org

To learn more about the history of the telecommunications industry.

How Telephones Work

http://www.howstuffworks.com/telephone.htm

Includes links to Bell's application for his patent and drawings and explanations of Bell's many experiments that led to the invention of the telephone.

Organization

Alexander Bell National Historic Site

P.O. Box 159

Baddeck, Nova Scotia Canada

(902) 295-2069

To learn more about Alexander Graham Bell and the invention of the telephone.

Index

About the Author

Patricia K. Kummer writes and edits nonfiction books for children and young adults from her home office in Lisle, Illinois. She has a master of arts degree in history from Marquette University in Milwaukee, Wisconsin. Before starting her career in publishing, she taught social studies at the junior high/middle school level. Since then, she has written about history for textbook publishers. She also has written six books (*Côte d'Ivoire*, *Ukraine*, *Tibet*, *Singapore*, *Cameroon*, and *Korea*) in the Children's Press series Enchantment of the World and two books (*Currency* and *The Calendar*) in the Franklin Watts series Inventions That Shaped the World. On a recent trip to New Mexico, Ms. Kummer had the pleasure of visiting the Telephone Pioneer Museum.